The Western Approaches

Howard Nemerov

The Western Approaches

Poems 1973-75

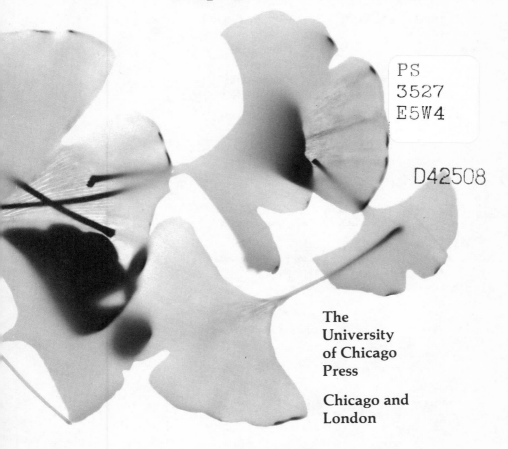

The
University
of Chicago
Press

Chicago and
London

The author would like
to thank the editors of
the following journals
for permission to
reprint poems first
appearing in their
pages:

American Poetry Review
American Scholar
Carleton Miscellany
Boston University Journal
Chicago Review
Georgia Review
New Republic
New Yorker
Poetry
Salmagundi
Sewanee Review

The University of Chicago Press, Chicago 60637
The University of Chicago Press, Ltd., London

Library of Congress Cataloging in Publication Data

Nemerov, Howard.
   The Western approaches.

   I. Title.
PS3527.E5W4   811'.5'4   75–5074
ISBN:0–226–57526–0

To Elbert Lenrow

Contents

1 **The Way**

Fugue 3
Late Late Show 4
The Doomsday Books 5
Strange Metamorphosis of Poets 6
Cosmic Comics 7
The Metaphysical Automobile 8
Watching Football on TV 10
Route Two 15
Ozymandias II 16
He 17
Two Pair 18
Nebuchadnezzar, Solus 19
Einstein & Freud & Jack 20
Waiting Rooms 22
Capitals 24
Critic 25
Novelists 26
Wolves in the Zoo 27
The Common Wisdom 28
The Western Approaches 29
A Memory of the War 31
To the Rulers 32
Boy with Book of Knowledge 34
Amnesty 36
Eve 38
Pockets 39
Hero with Girl and Gorgon 40
The Backward Look 41

2 The
Ground

The Dependencies   45
Figures of Thought   46
Late Summer   47
A Cabinet of Seeds Displayed   48
Flower Arrangements   49
Walking Down Westgate in the Fall   50
Ginkgoes in Fall   51
Again   52
The Consent   53
Equations of a Villanelle   54
A Common Saw   55
Near the Old People's Home   56
Nature Morte   57
Seeing Things   58
First Snow   59
Childhood (a translation of Rainer Maria
   Rilke's *Kindheit*)   60

3 The
Mind

Casting   65
Fiction   66
Reflexion of a Novelist   67
The Weather of the World   68
There   70
Nightmare   71
Exasperations of a Novelist   72
Learning the Trees   74
Conversing with Paradise   77
Playing the Inventions   78
The Measure of Poetry   82
The Four Ages   85
The Thought of Trees   88
Drawing Lessons   91
Du rêve, de la mathématique,
    et de la mort   95
Translation   96
Speculation   97
Gyroscope   98
Playing Skittles   99
TV   100
The Spy   101
The Old Days   102
Aftermath   103
The Banquet (a translation of Dante
    Alighieri's *Convito*, Dissertation 2,
    Canzone 1)   105
An Ending   108
Origin   109
Plane   110

1 The Way

According to our tradition, when a man dies there comes to him the Angel, who says: "Now I will tell you the secret of life and the meaning of the universe." One man to whom this happened said: "Take off, grey Angel. Where were you when I needed you?" Among all the hosts of the dead he is the only one who does not know the secret of life and the meaning of the universe; whence he is held in superstitious veneration by the rest.

Fugue

You see them vanish in their speeding cars,
The many people hastening through the world,
And wonder what they would have done before
This time of time speed distance, random streams
Of molecules hastened by what rising heat?
Was there never a world where people just sat still?

Yet they might be all of them contemplatives
Of a timeless now, drivers and passengers
In the moving cars all facing to the front
Which is the future, which is destiny,
Which is desire and desire's end—
What are they doing but just sitting still?

And still at speed they fly away, as still
As the road paid out beneath them as it flows
Moment by moment into the mirrored past;
They spread in their wake the parading fields of food,
The windowless works where who is making what,
The grey towns where the wishes and the fears are done.

Late Late Show

Movies, the Old Law. TV is the New
Wherein the dead who did our phantasies
Have stolen back into the living room
To do their thing again. Boxed in the bad
Resurrections of Hell, in a seamy air
And silver drizzle of shifting shape and shade,
Witnessed without terror and without pity,
Eternal return unrolls itself anew.

The stars and the members of unremembered casts
Are spared the selfish indifference of the selves
Kept up past bedtime by their early lives
Become our late ones, moving in a light
So swiftly scanning it can keep them up
As long as the old show stays on the road,
Addressing its advertisements for life
To us the living, while even their dead die.

The Doomsday Books

Nobody knows if the water will dry up
Before the air gives out or gets to be
Too thick to breathe in, whether we will die
Of traffic jam or cigarette or drug
Or bomb or plague transmitted through the air
By wingéd carriers at the speed of sound;
Inflation, famine, and fleets from outer space
Full of colonial imperialists from Mars
Are also considered among the candidates.

Meanwhile, the more lovers there are, the more
Consumers there will be, and increased food
Accelerates the fucking frequency
That multiplies the mouths over the food.
We can't win nor we can't even break even
At wearing out this world because we must.
On every front at once we reach the edge;
At least it seems that way to the middle class,
With Chicken Licken writing all these books.

Strange Metamorphosis of Poets

From epigram to epic is the course
For riders of the American wingéd horse.
They change both size and sex over the years,
The voice grows deeper and the beard appears;
Running for greatness they sweat away their salt,
They start out Emily and wind up Walt.

Cosmic Comics

There is in space a small black hole
Through which, say our astronomers,
The whole damn thing, the universe,
Must one day fall. That will be all.

Their shrinks can't get them to recall
How this apocalyptic dream
's elaborated on a humbler theme:
The toilet bowl, the Disposall.

Let prizes from the Privy Purse
Reward the Ultimate Hygiene
For flushing all flesh from the scene.

Where Moses saw the seat of God   Exod. 33. 23.
Science has seen what's just as odd,
The asshole of the universe.

7

The Metaphysical Automobile

I

It's abstract nouns, among the myths of mind,
Make most of the trouble. Where there used to be
Honest chimera and candid hippogriff,
Whom none did the disservice of belief,
We've Communism and Democracy,
Labor and Capital, and others of the kind;
Whole circus tents collapsed, whose shapeless terms
Cover the billow and bulge of fighting forms.

And pronouns, too. I, the erected vowel,
Stands up for a man's own lecherous will,
All right; but You already has become
Ambiguous, while We, They, Us and Them,
Four partners to a Freudian affair,
Conceal a con game and the threat of war.

II

You can't resolve a contradiction by
Getting between the warring opposites.
The idea of a car either has a dent
In its left front fender or it downright don't,
There's no third way. For on the roads of thought
You're either nominalist or realist,
The only question universals ask
Is is you is or is you ain't my baby?
And mild conceptualists, those innocent

Bystanders, stand to get hit from either side.
Accursed are the compromisers and
The sorry citizens of buffer states,
Nor fish nor flesh nor fowl nor good red herring,
And spued out by the Lamb, the great I Am.

III

In the eternal combustion engine, force
Is from the contradicting opposites,
And yet their warfare passes into play:
The pistons know that up opposes down,
Closed in their cylinders they cannot know
Around, and would not be converted by
The revelation of the wheel. So straight
Flat roads of logic lie about a globe
On which the shortest way between two points
Happens to be a curve. And so do song
And story, winding crank and widdershins,
Still get there first, and poetry remains
Eccentric and odd and riddling and right,
Eternal return of the excluded middle.

Watching Football on TV

I

It used to be only Sunday afternoons,
But people have got more devoted now
And maybe three four times a week retire
To their gloomy living room to sit before
The polished box alive with silver light
And moving shadows, that incessantly
Gives voice, even when pausing for messages.
The colored shadows made of moving light,
The voice that ritually recites the sense
Of what they do, enter a myriad minds.
Down on the field, massed bands perform the anthem
Sung by a soprano invisible elsewhere;
Sometimes a somewhat neutral public prayer—
For in the locker rooms already both
Sides have prayed God to give them victory.

II

Totemic scarabs, exoskeletal,
Nipped in at the thorax, bulky above and below,
With turreted hard heads and jutting masks
And emblems of the lightning or the beast;
About the size of beetles in our sight,
Save for the closeup and the distant view,
Yet these are men, our representatives
More formidable than ourselves in speed and strength
And preparation, and more injured too;

Bandage and cast exhibit breakages
Incurred in wars before us played before;
Hard plaster makes a weapon of an arm,
A calf becomes a club. Now solemnly
They take up their positions in the light,
And soon their agon will begin again.

III

To all this there are rules. The players must
Remember that in the good society
Grabbing at anybody's mask will be
A personal foul and incur a penalty.
So too will pushing, tripping, interfering
In any manner with someone else's pass.
Fighting is looked on with particular
Severity; though little harm can come
To people so plated at shoulder, head and thigh,
The most conspicuous offenders are
Ejected from the game and even fined.
That's one side of the coin, the other one
Will bear the picture of a charging bull
Or some such image imprecating fear,
And for its legend have the one word: *Kill.*

IV

Priam on one side sending forth eleven
Of many sons, and Agamemnon on

The other doing much the same; is it
The Game of Troy again? the noble youth
Fiery with emulation, maneuvering
Toward power and preeminence? Well no,
It's not. Money is the name of the game
From the board room to the beers and souvenirs.
The players are mean and always want more money.
The owners are mean and always have more money
And mean to keep it while the players go
Out there to make them more; they call themselves
Sportsmen, they own, are and carry a club.
Remember this when watching the quarterback's
Suppliant hands under the center's butt.

V

We watch all afternoon, we are enthralled
To what? some drama of the body and
The intellectual soul? of strategy
In its rare triumphs and frequent pratfalls?
The lucid playbook in the memory
Wound up in a spaghetti of arms and legs
Waving above a clump of trunks and rumps
That slowly sorts itself out into men?
That happens many times. But now and then
The runner breaks into the clear and goes,
The calm parabola of a pass completes
Itself like destiny, giving delight
Not only at skill but also at the sight

Of men who imitate necessity
By more than meeting its immense demands.

VI

Passing and catching overcome the world,
The hard condition of the world, they do
Human intention honor in the world.
A football wants to wobble, that's its shape
And nature, and to make it spiral true
's a triumph in itself, to make it hit
The patterning receiver on the hands
The instant he looks back, well, that's to be
For the time being in a state of grace,
And move the viewers in their living rooms
To lost nostalgic visions of themselves
As in an earlier, other world where grim
Fate in the form of gravity may be
Not merely overcome, but overcome
Casually and with style, and that is grace.

VII

Each year brings rookies and makes veterans,
They have their dead by now, their wounded as well,
They have Immortals in a Hall of Fame,
They have the stories of the tribe, the plays
And instant replays many times replayed.
But even fame will tire of its fame,

And immortality itself will fall asleep.
It's taken many years, but yet in time,
To old men crouched before the ikon's changes,
Changes become reminders, all the games
Are blended in one vast remembered game
Of similar images simultaneous
And superposed; nothing surprises us
Nor can delight, though we see the tight end
Stagger into the end zone again again.

Route Two

Along Route Two I saw a sign
Standing out in a swamp. One line
It spoke that might epitomize
The ambition of Free Enterprise:
Save While You Spend, is what it said
Across the swamp and to the road,
Save While You Spend. As if one saw
A way to beat the Second Law
By pouring money down the drain
As long as it was one's own drain.

Ozymandias II

I met a guy I used to know, who said:
"You take your '57 Karnak, now,
The model that they called their Coop de Veal
That had the pointy rubber boobs for bumpers—
You take that car, owned by a nigger now
Likelier'n not, with half its chromium teeth
Knocked down its throat and aerial ripped off,
Side stitched with like bullets where the stripping's gone
And rust like a fungus spreading on the fenders,

Well, what I mean, that fucking car still runs,
Even the moths in the upholstery are old
But it gets around, you see one on the street
Beat-up and proud, well, Jeezus what a country,
Where even the monuments keep on the move."

He

Slave to a God whose sole known verb is *Flatter*!
His world a spectre and his soul a wraith
Astray in the illusion he called *Matter*,
He got religion when he lost his faith.

Two Pair

More money's lost, old gamblers understand,
On two pair than on any other hand;

And in the great world that may be the cause
That we've two pair of First and Second Laws.

The first pair tells us we may be redeemed,
But in a world, the other says, that's doomed.

In one, the First Law says: Nothing is Lost.
The other First Law adds: But we are lost.

One Second Law fulfills what spake the prophets;
The other tersely states: There are no profits.

Baffled between the Old Law and the New,
What boots it to be told both sets are true,

Or that disorder in the universe
Is perfectly legal, and always getting worse?

Nebuchadnezzar, Solus

Seven years I had to think it over;
Or not to think, I couldn't, but to yield.
Seven years on all fours and in clover,
Taking a nosedown closeup of the field.

I understood the weather of the season,
Endured the pain, but not the *Angst*, of heaven,
And my dumb knowledge was relieved of reason
Till I, agreed with heaven, deemed us even.

I stood, I bathed, in glory was arrayed
And formal made submission to the Will
Above, though half my soul in secret prayed
To be my animal again and still.

But I forbid all men from making ballads
About my seven years spent browsing salads.

Einstein & Freud & Jack

to Allen Tate on his 75th Birthday

Death is a dead, at least that's what Freud said.
Long considering, he finally thought
Life but a detour longer or less long;
Maybe that's why the going gets so rough.

When Einstein wrote to ask him what he thought
Science might do for world peace, Freud wrote back:
Not much. And took the occasion to point out
That science too begins and ends in myth.

His myth was of the sons conspired together
To kill the father and share out his flesh,
Blood, power, women, and the primal guilt
Thereon entailed, which they must strive

Vainly to expiate by sacrifice,
Fixed on all generations since, of sons.
Exiled in London, a surviving Jew,
Freud died of cancer before the war began

That Einstein wrote to Roosevelt about
Advising the research be started that,
Come seven years of dying fathers, dying sons,
In general massacre would end the same.

Einstein. He said that if it were to do
Again, he'd sooner be a plumber. He
Died too. We live on sayings said in myths,
And die of them as well, or ill. That's that,

Of making many books there is no end,
And like it saith in the book before that one,
What God wants, don't you forget it, Jack,
Is your contrite spirit, Jack, your broken heart.

Waiting Rooms

What great genius invented the waiting room?
Every sublime idea no doubt is simple, but
Simplicity alone is never enough.
A cube sequestered in space and filled with time,
Pure time, refined, distilled, denatured time
Without qualities, without even dust . . .
Dust in a sunbeam between Venetian blinds
Where a boy and his mother wait . . . Eternity!
But I am straying from the subject: waiting rooms.

All over the globe, in the great terminals
And the tiny rooms of disbarred abortionists,
For transport, diagnosis, or divorce . . .
Alas! Maybe this mighty and terrible theme
Is too much for me. But wait! I have an idea.

You've heard it said, of course, that anything
May instantly turn into everything
In this world secreting figures of itself
Forever and everywhere? How wonderful
That is, how horrible. Wherever you wait,
Between anticipation and regret,
Between the first desire and the second
Is but the razor of a moment, is
Not even time; and neither is motion more,
At sixty miles an hour or six hundred,
Than an illusion sent by devils to afford

Themselves illusory laughs at our expense
(we suffer, but they become no happier).

Think how even in heaven where they wait
The Resurrection, even in the graves
Of heaven with the harps, this law applies:
One waiting room will get you to the next.
Even your room, even your very own,
With the old magazines on the end tables,
The goldfish in the bowl below the window
Where the sunbeam falls between Venetian blinds . . .
And in the downstairs hall there is your mailbox,
One among many gathering paper and dust,
A waiting room in figure, summing up
Much in a little, the legendary box
Where hope only remains. You wait and see.

Capitals

When a common noun becomes a Proper One
It seems to add an invisible *de* or *von*,
Gets uppity, forgets its former friends
And can't remember even what it means.

Look at intelligence. It went that way
As soon as ever it joined the CIA;
And the even dozen gods themselves turned odd
The minute they got upped in grade to God.

Critic

"I am self-evident," the mirror said,
"Plain as the nose on your face; plain as your face."

I unbelieving looked behind the glass
On razor, styptic, mouthwash and Band-aid;

And it has been my life's ambition since
To elucidate the mirror by its medicines.

Novelists

Theirs is a trade for egomaniacs,
People whose parents did not love them well.
It's done by wasps and women, Jews and Blacks,
In every isolation ward in Hell.

They spend their workadays imagining
What never happened and what never will
To people who are not and whose non-being
Always depends on the next syllable.

It's strange, and little wonder it makes them so
Whose lives are spun out talking to themselves
In allegories of themselves that go
Down on the paper like dividing cells

That form in communes and make colonies
And do each other in by love and hate
And generally enact the ceremonies
Intended to harmonize freedom and fate

Among the creatures and in the writer's soul.
The writer's *soul*? It's as if one abyss
Primps at the other's mirror and the whole
Shebang hangs fire while the lovers kiss.

Wolves in the Zoo

They look like big dogs badly drawn, drawn wrong.
A legend on their cage tells us there is
No evidence that any of their kind
Has ever attacked man, woman, or child.

Now it turns out there were no babies dropped
In sacrifice, delaying tactics, from
Siberian sleds; now it turns out, so late,
That Little Red Ridinghood and her Gran

Were the aggressors with the slavering fangs
And tell-tale tails; now it turns out at last
That grey wolf and timber wolf are near extinct,
Done out of being by the tales we tell

Told us by Nanny in the nursery;
Young sparks we were, to set such forest fires
As blazed from story into history
And put such bounty on their wolvish heads

As brought the few survivors to our terms,
Surrendered in happy Babylon among
The peacock dusting off the path of dust,
The tiger pacing in the stripéd shade.

The Common Wisdom

Their marriage is a good one. In our eyes
What makes a marriage *good*? Well, that the tether
Fray but not break, and that they stay together.
One should be watching while the other dies.

The Western Approaches

As long as we look forward, all seems free,
Uncertain, subject to the Laws of Chance,
Though strange that chance should lie subject to laws,
But looking back on life it is as if
Our Book of Changes never let us change.

Stories already told a time ago
Were waiting for us down the road, our lives
But filled them out; and dreams about the past
Show us the world is post meridian
With little future left to dream about.

Old stories none but scholars seem to tell
Among us any more, they hide the ways,
Old tales less comprehensible than life
Whence nonetheless we know the things we do
And do the things they say the fathers did.

When I was young I flew past Skerryvore
Where the Nine Maidens still grind Hamlet's meal,
The salt and granite grain of bitter earth,
But knew it not for twenty years and more.
My chances past their changes now, I know

How a long life grows ghostly towards the close
As any man dissolves in Everyman
Of whom the story, as it always did, begins
In a far country, once upon a time,
There lived a certain man and he had three sons . . .

A Memory of the War

Most what I know of war is what I learned
When mine was over and they shipped me home.
I'd been a chauffeur with the RAF
And didn't know the first damn thing about
The American way of doing anything
Till they told me I was Officer of the Day
(at midnight, yet) and gave me a whopping great
Blue automatic and sat me on D Deck
At the top of a ladder leading to a hold
Where a couple hundred enlisted men were sleeping,
And said I was to sit there till relieved.
"But what's this for?" I said about the gun,
And was answered: "If this ship shows any sign
Of going down, you shoot down the first son-
ofabitch sticks his head up through this hatch."
So that is what I did, and how I learned
About the War: I sat there till relieved.

To the Rulers

We read and hear about you every day,
What you decide we need, or want, or may
Be made to stand still for . . . Now let us pray.

Approaching the year One Thousand of Your Lord,
Men fixed that date for the ending of the world;
Truth and round numbers naturally in accord.

One of society's earlier ego trips,
That hinted only this to your Lordships:
A calendar implies apocalypse.

That passed. And all the reborn skeptics smiled
Over such fancies as could have beguiled
No one who was not but a simple child.

Now, as we near the next millennium,
Reality's caught up with Kingdom Come—
Why wait two dozen years to round the sum?

O Conscript Fathers, sponsors of the draft,
Prospective survivors on the little raft
That when the world sinks will be what is left,

I hear you praying, as your fingers trill
Unnervingly at night beside the pill,
The button, the hot line to the Other Will,

Your prayer, that used to be Caligula's too,
If they all only had one neck . . . It's so
Unnecessary and out of date. We do.

Boy with Book of Knowledge

He holds a volume open in his hands:
Sepia portraits of the hairy great,
The presidents and poets in their beards
Alike, simplified histories of the wars,
Conundrums, quizzes, riddles, games and poems,

"Immortal Poems"; at least he can't forget them,
Barbara Fritchie and the Battle Hymn,
And best of all America the Beautiful,
Whose platitudinous splendors ended with
"From sea to shining sea," and made him cry

And wish to be a poet, only to say such things,
From sea to shining sea. Could that have been
Where it began? the vast pudding of knowledge,
With poetry rare as raisins in the midst
Of those gold-lettered volumes black and green?

Mere piety to think so. But being now
As near his deathday as his birthday then,
He would acknowledge all he will not know,
The silent library brooding through the night
With all its lights continuing to burn

Insomniac, a luxury liner on what sea
Unfathomable of ignorance who could say?
And poetry, as steady, still, and rare
As the lighthouses now unmanned and obsolete
That used to mark America's dangerous shores.

Amnesty

The memory is not good. There is something loose
Inside the head, that is threatening the brain.
The past passes, that's all, it takes the pain.
I can't remember what happened to the Jews,

I can't remember Korea or Vietnam;
Now that a decade of rut and riot is out,
Replaced by a dumber time of rot and rout,
There are days I can't remember even the Bomb

Or the Cold War, or tell one Senator
McCarthy from another, or which came first;
I've forgotten what they call *our time*, and, worst,
Forgotten what they said it all was for.

I know it's for the best, there was too much pain,
Killing those children, bombing the Iron Age
Back into the Stone Age. When you're my age
You'll have learned forgiveness over and again:

Forgiveness forgets, and I forgive the lot,
Forgive my country and the world, forgive
Especially myself, that I may live;
But what I forgive us for I have forgot.

And that the future may be bright with loss
I'm driving the children to Pike's Peak to see
The big statue of Daddy Warbucks, where he
Is shown in the act of Putting Up the Cross.

Eve

There are no more shopping days to Christmas.
Slowly we wheel our wire cages down
And back along the fluorescent aisles,
And down and back again, prowling the maze
Of goods, by many musics played upon,
The glaze of obligation in our eyes
As we take in the dozen television sets
Tuned to the same Western, and the caged birds
No one has wanted to give, and the many
Remaining goldfish desperately marked down.

Come all ye faithful, calls the music now.
We march in time, stopping to take, put back,
And sometimes take again. We buy some rolls
Of merry wrapping paper, and push the whole
Caboodle to the counter where it's counted
And added up and put in paper bags
By the girl we pay and get the right change from
With some green stamps. She smiles, and we smile back.
A dollar bill is pinned to her left tit
Somewhere about the region of the heart.

Pockets

Are generally over or around
Erogenous zones, they seem to dive
In the direction of those

Dark places, and indeed
It is their nature to be dark
Themselves, keeping a kind

Of thieves' kitchen for the things
Sequestered from the world
For long or little while,

The keys, the handkerchiefs,
The sad and vagrant little coins
That are really only passing through.

For all they locate close to lust,
No pocket ever sees another;
There is in fact a certain sadness

To pockets, going their lonesome ways
And snuffling up their sifting storms
Of dust, tobacco bits and lint.

A pocket with a hole in it
Drops out; from shame, is that, or pride?
What is a pocket but a hole?

Hero with Girl and Gorgon

Child of the sunlight in the tower room,
When you have carried away Medusa's head,
When you have slain the dragon in the sea
And brought the maiden breathing from the rock
To be the bride, consider, wingéd man,
The things that went before and what things else
Must follow, when in the land beyond the North
The grey hags sang to you, the three grey hags
Sharing an eye and a tooth, dim-glimmering in
White darkness, sang to you their song of how
The things that were surpass the things that are . . .

As though the vision from that time reversed,
As in the glitter of the shield the sword
Cut backward in aversion from the cold
Brow's beauty and the wide unpitying gaze . . .

And now you must go onward through the world
With that great head swung by the serpents held
At lantern height before you, lighting your way
Past living images that mock or curse,
Till paralyzed to silence in the stone
They run unmoved on your undying doom.

The Backward Look

As once in heaven Dante looked back down
From happiness and highest certainty
To see afar the little threshing floor
That makes us be so fierce, so we look now
And with what difference from this stony place,
Our sterile satellite with nothing to do,
Not even water in the so-called seas.

No matter the miracles that brought us here,
Consider the end. Even the immense power
Of being bored we brought with us from home
As we brought all things else, even the golf
Balls and the air. What are we doing here,
Foreshadowing the first motels in space?
"They found a desert and they left the Flag."

From earth we prayed to heaven; being now
In heaven, we reverse the former prayer:
Earth of the cemeteries and cloudy seas,
Our small blue agate in the big black bag,
Earth mother of us, where we make our death,
Earth that the old man knocked on with his staff
Beseeching, "Leve moder, let me in,"

Hold us your voyagers safe in the hand
Of mathematics, grant us safe return
To where the food is, and the fertile dung,
To generation, death, decay; to war,
Gossip and beer, and bed whether warm or cold,
As from the heaven of technology
We take our dust and rocks and start back down.

2 The Ground

Natura in reticulum sua genera connexit,
non in catenam: homines non possunt nisi
catenam sequi, cum non plura simul
possint sermone exponere.

Nature knits up her kinds in a network, not
in a chain; but men can follow only by
chains because their language can't handle
several things at once.

—Albrecht von Haller

The Dependencies

This morning, between two branches of a tree
Beside the door, epeira once again
Has spun and signed his tapestry and trap.
I test his early-warning system and
It works, he scrambles forth in sable with
The yellow hieroglyph that no one knows
The meaning of. And I remember now
How yesterday at dusk the nighthawks came
Back as they do about this time each year,
Grey squadrons with the slashes white on wings
Cruising for bugs beneath the bellied cloud.
Now soon the monarchs will be drifting south,
And then the geese will go, and then one day
The little garden birds will not be here.
See how many leaves already have
Withered and turned; a few have fallen, too.
Change is continuous on the seamless web,
Yet moments come like this one, when you feel
Upon your heart a signal to attend
The definite announcement of an end
Where one thing ceases and another starts;
When like the spider waiting on the web
You know the intricate dependencies
Spreading in secret through the fabric vast
Of heaven and earth, sending their messages
Ciphered in chemistry to all the kinds,
The whisper down the bloodstream: it is time.

Figures of Thought

To lay the logarithmic spiral on
Sea-shell and leaf alike, and see it fit,
To watch the same idea work itself out
In the fighter pilot's steepening, tightening turn
Onto his target, setting up the kill,
And in the flight of certain wall-eyed bugs
Who cannot see to fly straight into death
But have to cast their sidelong glance at it
And come but cranking to the candle's flame—

How secret that is, and how privileged
One feels to find the same necessity
Ciphered in forms diverse and otherwise
Without kinship—that is the beautiful
In Nature as in art, not obvious,
Not inaccessible, but just between.

It may diminish some our dry delight
To wonder if everything we are and do
Lies subject to some little law like that;
Hidden in nature, but not deeply so.

Late Summer

Look up now at what's going on aloft—
Not in high heaven, only overhead,
Yet out of reach of, unaffected by,
The noise of history and the newsboy's cry.

There grow the globes of things to come,
There fruits and futures have begun to form
Solid and shadowy along the boughs:
Acorns in neat berets, horse chestnuts huge
And shiny as shoes inside their spiny husks,
Prickly planets among the sweetgum's starry leaves.

So secretly next year secretes itself
Within this one, as far on forested slopes
The trees continue quietly making news,
Enciphering in their potencies of pulp
The matrix of much that hasn't happened yet.

A Cabinet of Seeds Displayed

These are the original monies of the earth,
In which invested, as the spark in fire,
They will produce a green wealth toppling tall,
A trick they do by dying, by decay,
In burial becoming each his kind
To rise in glory and be magnified
A million times above the obscure grave.

Reader, these samples are exhibited
For contemplation, locked in potency
And kept from act for reverence's sake.
May they remind us while we live on earth
That all economies are primitive;
And by their reservations may they teach
Our governors, who speak of husbandry
And think the hurricane, where power lies.

Flower Arrangements

for Pat

The flowers that a friend brings twice a week
Or even oftener accumulate
In plastic cups beside me on the table.
Not only I forget to throw them out,
But also I've a curiosity,
Fading a bit myself, to watch them fade.
They do it with much delicacy and style.

Shrinking into themselves, they keep their cool
And colors many days, their drying and
Diminishing would be imperceptible
But for the instance of the followers
Arranged beside them in the order of
Their severance and exile from the earth;
In death already though they know it not.

At last the petals shrivel, fold and fall,
The colors grow pastel and pale, the stems
Go brittle and the green starts turning brown;
The fireworks are over, and life sinks
Down in or else evaporates, but where?
From time to time I throw a cup away,
Wondering where lives go when they go out.

Walking Down Westgate in the Fall

The weather's changes are the private rites
And secret celebrations of the soul
So widely now believed not to exist.
The first clear autumn day, the summer rain,
The sudden fall of winter and the dark
When Daylight Saving goes, the sunny melt
Of several February days, to these
Changes the soul with changes of its own
And overtones responds in resonance.

Down Westgate, in the Fall, the housewives set
Chrysanthemums in bronze or marble bowls
Forth on the stoops, defying ice and snow
With their lion's mane, sun's face ruddy glow of gold.

Things like that marry weather with the soul,
Which would have its seasons if it did exist,
And sing its songs among the falling leaves
Under the autumn rain, and celebrate
Its mass with hymns and litanies of change,
Walking down Westgate past chrysanthemums,
Consenting with the winter soon to come,
Hearing the acorns bang on the roofs of cars
And bounce and roll along the rainy street.

Ginkgoes in Fall

They are the oldest living captive race,
Primitive gymnosperms that in the wild
Are rarely found or never, temple trees
Brought down in line unbroken from the deep
Past where the Yellow Emperor lies tombed.

Their fallen yellow fruit mimics the scent
Of human vomit, the definite statement of
An attitude, and their translucency of leaf,
Filtering a urinary yellow light,
Remarks a delicate wasting of the world,

An innuendo to be clarified
In winter when they defecate their leaves
And bear the burden of their branches up
Alone and bare, dynastic diagrams
Of their distinguished genealogies.

Again

Again, great season, sing it through again
Before we fall asleep, sing the slow change
That makes October burn out red and gold
And color bleed into the world and die,
And butterflies among the fluttering leaves
Disguise themselves until the few last leaves
Spin to the ground or to the skimming streams
That carry them along until they sink,
And through the muted land, the nevergreen
Needles and mull and duff of the forest floor,
The wind go ashen, till one afternoon
The cold snow cloud comes down the intervale
Above the river on whose slow black flood
The few first flakes come hurrying in to drown.

The Consent

Late in November, on a single night
Not even near to freezing, the ginkgo trees
That stand along the walk drop all their leaves
In one consent, and neither to rain nor to wind
But as though to time alone: the golden and green
Leaves litter the lawn today, that yesterday
Had spread aloft their fluttering fans of light.

What signal from the stars? What senses took it in?
What in those wooden motives so decided
To strike their leaves, to down their leaves,
Rebellion or surrender? and if this
Can happen thus, what race shall be exempt?
What use to learn the lessons taught by time,
If a star at any time may tell us: *Now.*

Equations of a Villanelle

The breath within us is the wind without,
In interchange unnoticed all our lives.
What if the same be true of world and thought?

Air is the ghost that comes and goes uncaught
Through the great system of lung and leaf that sieves
The breath within us and the wind without;

And utterance, or inspiration going out,
Is borne on air, on empty air it lives
To say the same is true of world and thought.

This is the spirit's seamless fabric wrought
Invisible, whose working magic gives
The breath within us to the wind without.

O great wind, blow through us despite our doubt,
Distilling all life's sweetness in the hives
Where we deny the same to world and thought,

Till death, the candle guttering to naught,
Sequesters every self as it forgives
The breath within us for the wind without;
What if the same be true of world and thought?

A Common Saw

Good king, that must approve the common saw,
Thou out of heaven's benediction comest
To the warm sun!
King Lear, 2.2.156-8

Had God but made me a religious man
I'd have it made. The suburb where I live
Affords an ample choice of synagogues
And seven different Christianities—

I'd go to all of them, to every one
In turn, continuous performances:
Confession and yarmulka, incense, candlelight,
High, low, and broad, reform and orthodox,

Allowing God no possible way out
But my salvation—save that God did not
Make me a religious man, but left me here,
From heaven's blessing come to the warm sun,

Twined round the pinkie and pinned under the thumb
Of Dame Kind dear and beautiful and dumb.

Near the Old People's Home

The people on the avenue at noon,
Sharing the sparrows and the wintry sun,
The turned-off fountain with its basin drained
And cement benches etched with checkerboards,

Are old and poor, most every one of them
Wearing some decoration of his damage,
Bandage or crutch or cane; and some are blind,
Or nearly, tap-tapping along with white wands.

When they open their mouths, there are no teeth.
All the same, they keep on talking to themselves
Even while bending to hawk up spit or blood
In gutters that will be there when they are gone.

Some have the habit of getting hit by cars
Three times a year; the ambulance comes up
And away they go, mumbling even in shock
The many secret names they have for God.

Nature Morte

Bees forage where the blue ajuga's grown
To make low forest of the sloping lawn,
A hummingbird on wings invisible
Kneels in the air before a lily's bell
Beneath the waving grove where light and shade
Their play among the latticed leaves have made.

Whatever the ostensive scene may be,
The painter studies its solemnity,
A stillness out of moving Nature carved,
The silence of the object unobserved.
That is what looks at us from those flat rooms
That hang in galleries like Time's own tombs.

The eye takes oriole and tanager,
A fountain's lazy splashing takes the ear,
While high above and slow across the sky
The tumbling-turreted galleon clouds go by
As Constable caught them doing long ago
Over the silent park at Wivenhoe.

Seeing Things

Close as I ever came to seeing things
The way the physicists say things really are
Was out on Sudbury Marsh one summer eve
When a silhouetted tree against the sun
Seemed at my sudden glance to be afire:
A black and boiling smoke made all its shape.

Binoculars resolved the enciphered sight
To make it clear the smoke was a cloud of gnats,
Their millions doing such a steady dance
As by the motion of the many made the one
Shape constant and kept it so in both the forms
I'd thought to see, the fire and the tree.

Strike through the mask? you find another mask,
Mirroring mirrors by analogy
Make visible. I watched till the greater smoke
Of night engulfed the other, standing out
On the marsh amid a hundred hidden streams
Meandering down from Concord to the sea.

First Snow

for Ian McHarg

Always the solemnest moment of the year
Is this one, when the few first flakes
Come falling, flying, riding down the wind
And minute upon minute multiply
To being blind and blinding myriads.

It used to be said that when the sun burns down,
Being after all a mediocre star
Of the main sequence, mortal as ourselves,
One snow will seal the sleepy cities up,
Filling their deep and canyoned avenues

Forever. That will be the day. And for all
I know it may be true; at least it was
One vulgarized version of the The Second Law
A century ago, and almost all
The celebrated authors did it up,

A natural: "London, Peking, Moscow, Rome,
Under their cerements of eternal snow,"
And so on; writing was a powerful stuff
Back then, and tales of entropy and The End
Could always snow the middle class. Meanwhile,
It only hisses through the whitening grass,
And rattles among the few remaining leaves.

59

Childhood

A translation of Rainer Maria Rilke's *Kindheit*
("Da rinnt der Schule lange Angst und Zeit . . .")

So ran the schoolday, full of time and stress
And waiting, full of stupid public sound.
O loneliness, O time too much to spend . . .
At last let out: through streets all clean and gay,
And through the plazas where the fountains play,
And gardens where the world seemed to expand.
And through all this in one's own little dress,
Other than others in their otherness—:
O strangest time, O time too much to spend,
O loneliness.

And through all this to see so far and deep:
The men, the women; the men, women, children
All in their otherness so well wrapped up;
And here and there a house, and now a hound
(and fear becoming trust without a sound)—:
O senseless sorrow, dreadful as in sleep,
O groundless deep.

And then to games: with ball and ring and hoop
There in a garden growing twilight grey;
And sometimes brushing against a grown-up,
Blind and unheeding in the haste of play . . .
And then at dusk, with prim and proper step
To walk back home, hand in a hand's firm grip—:
O ever more uncomprehended fate,
O fear, great weight.

And hours long beside the great grey lake
Kneeling to watch one's little sailboat bear
Away and be lost among so many other there
Taller and costlier, that crossed her wake;
And then to have to think of that small, bleak
Child's face, drowning still mirrored in that lake—:
O childhood, O likeness drawn to disappear.
But where? But where?

3 The Mind

Poetry, Painting & Music, the three Powers in Man of conversing with Paradise, which the flood did not Sweep away.

—William Blake

Casting

The waters deep, the waters dark,
Reflect the seekers, hide the sought,
Whether in water or in air to drown.
Between them curls the silver spark,
Barbed, baited, waiting, of a thought—
Which in the world is upside down,
The fish hook or the question mark?

Fiction

The people in the elevator all
Face front, they all keep still, they all
Look up with the rapt and stupid look of saints
In paintings at the numbers that light up
By turn and turn to tell them where they are.
They are doing the dance, they are playing the game.

To get here they have gone by avenue
And street, by ordinate and abscissa, and now
By this new coordinate, up. They are three-
dimensional characters, taken from real life;
They have their fates, whether to rise or fall,
And when their numbers come up they get out.

Reflexion of a Novelist

In time, these people all will know each other.
But me they will not know, spelling the words
Of which alone they will be put together
A certain while, though sundered afterwards.

Is happiness illusory or real?
I need not decide today, but should do soon.
Will meningitis or the automobile
Doom one or both, or should the honeymoon

End in the faced despair of their mistake?
Whichever, they cannot know me hovering there
A dimension past the space in which they speak
And do as they are told, nor be aware,
Even when bound and put upon the shelf,
How their voyeur will have exposed himself.

The Weather of the World

Now that the cameras zero in from space
To view the earth entire, we know the whole
Of the weather of the world, the atmosphere,
As though it were a great sensorium,
The vast enfolding cortex of the globe,
Containing contradictions, tempers, moods,
Able to be serene, gloomy or mad,
Liable to huge explosions, brooding in
Depressions over several thousand miles
In length and trailing tears in floods of sorrow
That drown the counties and the towns. What power
There is in feeling! We are witness to,
Enslaved beneath, the passions of a beast
Of water and air, a shaman shifting shape
At the mercy of his moods, trying to bend,
Maybe, but under pressure like to break.

His mind is our mind and the world's alike,
His smiles, his rages and aridities,
Reflect us large across the continents
And improvise our inwardness upon
The desert and the sea; we suffer him
As if he were the sufferer buried in
The self and hidden in heaven's indifference;
And like us he seeks balances that are
Inherently unstable to either hand;

The id, the superego, and the god
Of this world, the apparent devil of the will
Whom God has given power over us
Or cannot or else will not bring to heel,
Our nourisher and need, our sorrow and rage,
Reacting and reflecting on our lives
In windy eloquence and rainy light
As in the brilliant stillness of the sun.

There

Sacred is secret: at the confluence
Where the unclean, the holy, the forbidden,
Mingle their currents, there where mind and sense,
An inch behind the eyes, perform their hidden

And common ministry, turning a storm
Of photons into this world of trees and rocks
And stars and faces, not to forget the worm
That dieth not, back there in the black box

That listens for what's said between the ears,
The eavesdropper under the thatch, there is the place
Of power, the transformer bathed in blood
Dreaming its figures of a universe
Where all except a mirror's understood:
Disguise of devil and god, the human face.

Nightmare

When the grey stranger shows up in your dream,
Drawing his silken cord across your throat
To waken you while you die, and you hear your scream
Strangled behind you as you flee from him,

The other time, continuing yesterday,
Takes over with its watchful face aglow,
Its hands that go on scissoring away
Both worlds at once; and sweating cold you say

"I just got out in time." But that's not so,
As waking from a dark to a dark you know
That if you were for a time in mortal danger,
And are so still, it was not from a stranger.

Exasperations of a Novelist

I

Locked in the dictionary on the table,
The people of my book, except their names,
Lie dormant, waiting for an author able
To rearrange them from their anagrams.

For that great slumber is unconscious of
Every last word that anyone can say
About them and about their doings unto love
And unto death, the tome that starts at A

And keeps in the confusion of its dream
Bible and bibliothèque before it wakes
To the last buzzing of the Z, the sum
Of follies, knowledges, wisdoms and mistakes,

Myth of the order of the alphabet,
Chaos enciphered, of all sets the set.

II

Now hear this, all you people of my book,
You are a stubborn and a stiff-neck'd lot.
What is all this about your freedom? Look,
Once more, will you try to follow the plot?

Free will, in moderation, after all,
Is one thing, you can choose your suits and ties
And have what you like to eat. But when I call
For one of you to die, and no one dies,

That's serious. I'll give you a chapter more,
And that's the end: it will be suicide
For Jane and marriage among the other four—
Which way you pair your freedom shall decide.

But they go on as if they never heard
The Let There Be of my creating word.

Learning the Trees

Before you can learn the trees, you have to learn
The language of the trees. That's done indoors,
Out of a book, which now you think of it
Is one of the transformations of a tree.

The words themselves are a delight to learn,
You might be in a foreign land of terms
Like samara, capsule, drupe, legume and pome,
Where bark is papery, plated, warty or smooth.

But best of all are the words that shape the leaves—
Orbicular, cordate, cleft and reniform—
And their venation—palmate and parallel—
And tips—acute, truncate, auriculate.

Sufficiently provided, you may now
Go forth to the forests and the shady streets
To see how the chaos of experience
Answers to catalogue and category.

Confusedly. The leaves of a single tree
May differ among themselves more than they do
From other species, so you have to find,
All blandly says the book, "an average leaf."

Example, the catalpa in the book
Sprays out its leaves in whorls of three
Around the stem; the one in front of you
But rarely does, or somewhat, or almost;

Maybe it's not catalpa? Dreadful doubt.
It may be weeks before you see an elm
Fanlike in form, a spruce that pyramids,
A sweetgum spiring up in steeple shape.

Still, *pedetemtim* as Lucretius says,
Little by little, you do start to learn;
And learn as well, maybe, what language does
And how it does it, cutting across the world

Not always at the joints, competing with
Experience while cooperating with
Experience, and keeping an obstinate
Intransigence, uncanny, of its own.

Think finally about the secret will
Pretending obedience to Nature, but
Invidiously distinguishing everywhere,
Dividing up the world to conquer it,

And think also how funny knowledge is:
You may succeed in learning many trees
And calling off their names as you go by,
But their comprehensive silence stays the same.

Conversing with Paradise

for Robert Jordan

To see the world the way a painter must,
Responsive to distances, alive to light,
To changes in the colors of the day,
His mind vibrating at every frequency
He finds before him, from wind waves in wheat
Through trees that turn their leaves before the storm,
To the string-bag pattern of the pebbled waves
Over the shallows of the shelving cove
In high sunlight; and to the greater wave-
lengths of boulder and building, to the vast
Majestic measures of the mountain's poise;

And from these modulations of the light
To take the elected moment, silence it
In oils and earths beneath the moving brush,
And varnish it and put it in a frame
To seal it off as privileged from time,
And hang it for a window on the wall,
A window giving on the ever-present past;

How splendid it would be to be someone
Able to do these mortal miracles
In silence and solitude, without a word.

Playing the Inventions

Forthright instruction, wherewith lovers of the clavier, especially those desirous of learning, are shown in a clear way not only (1) to play two voices clearly, but also after further progress (2) to deal correctly and well with three obbligato parts, moreover at the same time to obtain not only good ideas, but also to carry them out well, but most of all to achieve a cantabile style of playing, and thereby to acquire a strong foretaste of composition. Prepared by Joh. Seb. Bach, Capellmeister to his Serene Highness the Prince of Anhalt-Cothen. Anno Christi 1723.

I

The merest nub of a notion, nothing more
Than a scale, a shake, a broken chord, will do
For openers; originality
Is immaterial, it is not the tune
But the turns it takes you through, the winding ways
Where both sides and the roof and floor are mirrors
With some device that will reflect in time
As mirrors do in space, so that each voice
Says over what the others say, because
Consideration should precede consent;
And only being uninformative
Will be the highest reach of wisdom known
In the perfect courtesy of music, where
The question answers only to itself
And the completed round excludes the world.

II

How arbitrary it must be, the sound
That breaks the silence; yet its valency,
Though hidden still, is great for other sounds
Drawn after it into the little dance
Prefigured in its possibilities:
The tune's not much until it's taken up.
O mystery of mind, that cannot know
Except by modeling what it would know,
Repeating accident to make it fate:
This is the thread that spins the labyrinth,
The acorn opened that unfolds the oak,
Word that holds space and sequence in the seed,
That splits the silence and divides the void
In phrases that reflect upon themselves,
To be known that way and not in paraphrase.

III

Is is a heartless business, happiness,
It always is. Two hundred and fifty years
Of time's wild wind that whips at the skin of that sea
Whose waves are men, two hundred and fifty years
Of a suffering multiplied as many times
As there were children born to give it form
By feeding it their bodies, minds and souls;
And still the moment of this music is,

Whether in merry or in melancholy mode,
A happiness implacable and austere,
The feeling that specifically belongs
To music when it heartlessly makes up
The order of its lovely, lonely world
Agreeing justice with surprise, the world
We play forever at while keeping time.

IV

Landowska said, to end an argument,
"Why don't you go on playing Bach your way
And let me play Bach his way?" putting down
Whoever-it-was forever; music's not
All harmony, Landowska too is dead,
Spirit acerb, though her records remain
Hermetically kept where time not much corrupts
Nor quite so quick. In our advancing age
Not only the effigy can be preserved
But the sound as well, only without the self,
As evanescent as it ever was.
At last even the inventions lock us out,
We go while they remain. The argument ends.
It's like a myth about inventing death:
We don't become immortal, but it does.

V

Ach, dear Bach, so beautiful a day!
A small breeze shakes the shadows of the leaves
Over the instrument, across your page,
Sprinklings of drops at the outer edge of spray
In patterns overpatterning your own.
And one sits here, "lover of the clavier
And desirous to learn," your backward dilettante,
Amateur, stumbling slowly through your thoughts
Where five and twenty decades of the world's
Sorrow and wrath are for a while as though
Dissolved in the clear streams of your songs
Whose currents twine, diverge, and twine again,
Seeming to think themselves about themselves
Like fountains flowering in their fall. Dear Bach,
It's a great privilege. It always is.

The Measure of Poetry

Consider the breaking of waves on a shore. The measure governing this movement is the product of a number of forces, some constant or relatively constant, others which vary somewhat, still others extremely variable or even, so far as concerns their periodicity, accidental: the tides, the length of travel of the waves, the angle and underwater topography of the shore, and the winds, both the great winds from far away and the local land and sea breezes.

The idea one gets from these waves, whether the sea is rough or calm, is the idea of a great consistency coupled with a great freakishness, absolute law consisting with absolute rage. The tide, drawn mainly by the mass of the moon, is slow and stable, a vast breathing-in-sleep, and yet, however, eccentrically offset to the revolution of the earth by somewhat more than an hour a day, in a long rhythmic cycle bringing the ebb and the flood by times to every instant. The force which generates the wave begins, perhaps, far away in mid-ocean, but it is not *that* water which ultimately strikes the shore; if you look at wave motion out at sea, where it is not affected by the bottom, you notice that most of the water going to the crest, if it is not torn off in spray up there, slides back the way it came. It is the power, not the material, which is transmitted. The wave begins to form, as a substantial body with its own history and fate, when its base meets with the slope of the shore; the resultant of the two opposed forces produces the high and rolling form. Either the wave rises until the unstable top curls forward and smashes down, or it rises steadily until the breaker is extruded at mid-height of the wave by pressure from above and below at once; this latter sort, because it throws its force forward rather than down, is less spectacular than the other, but it reaches further up the shore. The sum of these conflicting, cooperating powers, with the prevailing wind, generates individual forms and moments of great charm too complex to be analysed except in a general way, and as unpredictable in their particularity as the rainbow which sometimes glimmers in the spray blown from the falling crest.

The measure of poetry, too, begins far from the particular conformation of the poem, far out in the sea of tradition and the mind, even in the physiological deeps, where some empty, echoing, abstract interval begins to beat; it is the angle of incidence of this measure upon the materials of the poem which produces in the first place what in the result will be called "form." This tidal, surging element has to do with the general shape of the poem, and is a prior musical imposition upon its thought—musical, in that it exists at its beginning independently of any identifiable content: it is the power, not the material, which is transmitted. The poem is a quantity of force expended, like any human action, and is therefore not altogether formless even to begin with, but limited in its cadence by the energies present at its generation.

The rise of the shore shapes the wave. The objects which are to appear in the poem, as they begin to rise beneath the empty periodicity of the pure rhythm, introduce into that rhythm a new character, somewhat obstinate, angular, critical. But in another sense, which technically may be the more useful of the two, the analogy represents the elements of speech itself. The tidal impulse from far away, the wind's generation of force without content, these are the vowels; the consonants are rock and reed and sand, and the steep or shallow slope which gives the wave its form while absorbing the shock of its force, from strength bringing forth sweetness.

The laws of this measure are simple and large, so that in the scope of their generality room may remain for moments of freedom, moments of chaos; the complex conjunction itself raising up iridescences and fantastic shapes, relations which it may be that number alone could enrage into being.

The Four Ages

The first age of the world was counterpoint,
Music immediate to all the senses
Not yet exclusive in their separate realms,
Wordlessly weaving the tapestried cosmos
Reflected mosaic in the wakening mind.

That world was lost, though echoes of it stray
On every breeze and breath, fragmented and
Heard but in snatches, thenceforth understood
Only by listeners like Pythagoras,
Who held the music of the spheres was silence
Because we had been hearing it from birth,
And Shakespeare, who made his Caliban recite
Its praises in the temporary isle.

A second age. Hard consonants began
To interrupt the seamless river of sound,
Set limits, break up and define in bits
What had before been pure relationship.
Units arose, and separations; words
Entered the dancing-space and made it song.
Though the divine had gone, yet there was then
The keenest human intuition of
Its hiding from us one dimension past
What the five senses could receive or send.

In the third age, without our noticing
The music ceased to sound, and we were left
As unaccompanied and strangely alone,
Like actors suddenly naked in a dream.
Yet we had words, and yet we had the word
Of poetry, a thinner music, but
Both subtle and sublime in its lament
For all that was lost to all but memory.

The fourth age is, it always is, the last.
The sentences break ranks, the orchestra
Has left the pit, the curtain has come down
Upon the smiling actors, and the crowd
Is moving toward the exits through the aisles.
Illusion at last is over, all proclaim
The warm humanity of common prose,
Informative, pedestrian and plain,
Imperative and editorial,
Opinionated and proud to be so,
Delighted to explain, but not to praise.

This is not history, it is a myth.
It's *de rigueur* for myths to have four ages,
Nobody quite knows why, unless to match
Four seasons and four elements and four
Voices of music and four gospels and four
Cardinal points on the compass rose and four
Whatever elses happen to come in four.

These correspondences are what remain
Of the great age when all was counterpoint
And no one minded that nothing mattered or meant.

The Thought of Trees

It is a common fancy that trees are somehow conscious
and stand as the silent or whispering witnesses of the ways
in which we bustle through the world. But it is a truth of
poetical imagination that the trees are guardians and
sponsoring godfathers of a great part of thought. Not
merely that various traditions have looked on trees as
sacred figures of the cosmos, as the source of moral
distinctions, as bearing all golden things, the apples, the
bough, the fleece; but also that trees, more than we
generally allow, have formed our view of the creation and
nature of things, and, ambiguously responsible for these,
the mind's image of its own process. This we are told by
metaphors: a family tree, the root of the matter, a
trunkline, a branch of the subject, and so on.

Trees appear as the formative image behind much
thought brought to the critical point of paradox—

Where order in variety we see,
And where, though all things differ, all agree,

as Pope politely says of Windsor Forest. That trees, the
largest of living things, are initially contained in tiny
seeds, is already a spectacularly visible legend of the
mysteries of generation and death. The tree, rooted in
earth and flowering in heaven, intimates obscure and
powerful reflexive propositions about the two realms; that
root and top strangely mirror one another deepens and
complicates the human analogy. The relation of single
trunk and manifold branches forms the pattern for

meditation on the one and the many, cause and effect, generality and particulars; while the movement in three stages, from many roots through one trunk to many branches, is supremely the image of historical process. The tree's relation with its leaves translates the paradigm into temporal terms, speaking of individual, generation, race, of identity continuous in change, of mortal endurance threaded through mortal evanescence, of times and a time.

Trees imagine life, and our imaginations follow as they may. The growth of a tree, its synchronous living and dying, from soft shoot to implacably hard (still growing) wood; the vast liquid transactions of capillarity within the solid form; the hard bark which nevertheless, as in the elm, reminds of water in its twisting flow; the enduring image of fluid life recorded in the rivery grain of boards (a mystical saying:—"Split the stick and there is Jesus"); the generalized simplicity composed of multitudinous complexity, generalized symmetry from the chaotic scrawl of upper branches; the simultaneity of freedom and order, richness and elegance, chance and destiny—these are some of the imaginings of the trees, which out of the earth and the air have dreamed so much of the human mind.

As architectural forms reflect their material origins, the first columns having been trees, so also with the mind. And so perhaps with its conclusions? "I shall be like that tree," Swift said to Edward Young, "I shall die first at the top." Since the eighteenth century, anyhow, when cathedrals began to remind people of forests and forests of cathedrals, it has come to seem sometimes that the mind acts in a drama staged with so high a regard for *realism* that the trees on the scene are carpentered at considerable cost out of real wood. Still, dryads and dendrones, the trees are within us, having their quiet irrefutable say about what we are and may become; how they are one of the shapes of our Protean nature, Melville in a single line expresses best—

The hemlock shakes in the rafter, the oak in the driving keel

—and it is the founding tenet of poetical imagination that such images are inexhaustibly speaking, they call to compelling, strange analogies all thought that flowers in its fact.

Drawing Lessons

I

Your pencil will do particles and waves—
We call them points and lines—and nothing else.
Today we shall explore the mystery
Of points and lines moving over the void—
We call it paper—to imitate the world.
First think a moment of the ocean wave
When it stubs its toe against the scend of the shore
And stumbles forward, somersaults and breaks.
A moment ago nothing was there but wave,
And now nothing is here but particles;
So point and line not only turn into
Each other, but each hides from the other, too.
The seed of a point grows into a tree of line,
The line unfolding generates the plane
Of the world, perspective space in light and shade.

II

The points and lines, the seashore and the sea,
The particles and waves, translate as well
Into the consonants and vowels that make
The speech that makes the world; a simple thing.
Or else a complex thing proceeding still
From simple opposites that make it seem
As if it might be understood, though this
Is probably illusion in the sense,

Delusion in the mind, making the world
Our true hallucination. Much as matter
And anti-matter are said to explode at touch,
So at the meeting-place of sea, air, shore,
Both sides explode, the ocean into spray,
The shore more slowly into boulders, rocks,
And final sand. All this repeats itself.

III

Always repeat yourself. To draw a line
's not much, but twenty-seven wavy lines
In parallel will visibly become
The sea; by tempering their distances
Apart, now near, now far away, we make
Ranges of mountains standing in their valleys;
By arbitrary obstacles of shape
That will prohibit passage to our lines,
We make a fleet of sailboats or a forest,
Depending on what shapes we have left void.
We see that repetition makes the world
The way it is, Nature repeats herself
Indefinitely in every kind, and plays
Far-ranging variations on the kinds,
Doodling inventions endlessly, as the pencil does.

IV

We said the water and the shore explode
And then repeat; that's not quite the whole truth.
For water has the wondrous property
And power of assembling itself again
When shattered, but the shore cannot do that.
The Second Law seems to reverse itself
For water, but not for land, whose massive cliffs
Break into boulders that break into rocks
That then descend to sand and don't return.
While I've been talking, you've been drawing lines
With your pencil, illustrating what I say
Along with whatever else you illustrate:
The pencil lead's become a stub, its black
Graphite remains became the world you made,
And it will shorten when you sharpen it.

V

The Second Law's an instrument, we're told,
Of immense power, but there's sorrow in it,
The invention of a parsimonious people
Accustomed to view creation on a budget
Cut to economy more than delight
At splendor overflowing every vessel.
Land is the locus of form and dignity
Disguising the way down to age and death,

Shameful decay, and dust that blows away—
See, rub your drawing and it smudges into dust,
Because your pencil is a citizen
Of the middle class material world, designed
To be a minor illustrator of
What we become and what becomes of us.
The sea's a little more mysterious than that.

Du rêve, de la mathématique, et de la mort

On dreams, on mathematics, and on death.
Card-catalogues turn up such heady stuff
Sometimes as this, this rapture from the depths
Which isn't where it should be on the shelf.
For a moment, remembering Borges' poor young clerk,
I idly consider writing it myself,
Setting a record for the shortest work
The world had ever seen on three such themes
Of such import as death and math and dreams.

I think of asking that a search be made,
But give it up, my French is not so great
And right now I've got plenty on my plate
Without this title turned up by pure chance
As if designed to bait my ignorance.
And yet—? But I shall let this once-glimpsed fish
Swim through the deep of thought beyond my wish,
And resign myself to knowing nothing more
Du rêve, de la mathématique, et de la mort.

Translation

Anima quodammodo omnia,
How lovely and exact the fit between
The language and the thing it means to say.
In English all but the sense evaporates:
The soul is in a manner all there is.
What's that but a poor thin mingy thing
Fit for the brain alone? Where is that world,
Where did it go, in which they said those things
And sang those things in their high halls of stone?
Vanished utterly, and we have instead
The world is everything that is the case,
That's flat enough to satisfy no one
After the lonely longings of plainsong:
In paradisum deducant te angeli,
What's that in other syllables and modes,
Now angels lead thee into paradise?
It still may draw a tremor and a tear
Sometimes, if only for its being gone,
That untranslatable, translated world
Of the Lady and the singers and the dead.

Speculation

Prepare for death. But how can you prepare
For death? Suppose it isn't an exam,
But more like the Tavern Scene in Henry IV,
Or that other big drunk, the Symposium?

Remember, everybody will be there,
Sooner or later at first, then all at once.
Maybe the soul at death becomes a star.
Maybe the galaxies are one great dance,

Maybe. For as earth's population grows,
So does the number of the unfixed stars,
Exploding from the sempiternal Rose
Into the void of an expanding universe.

If it be so, it doesn't speak well for
The social life hereafter: faster than light
The souls avoid each other, as each star
Speeds outward, goes out, or goes out of sight.

Gyroscope

This admirable gadget, when it is
Wound on a string and spun with steady force,
Maintains its balance on most any smooth
Surface, pleasantly humming as it goes.
It is whirled not on a constant course, but still
Stands in unshivering integrity
For quite some time, meaning nothing perhaps
But being something agreeable to watch,
A silver nearly silence gleaning a still-
ness out of speed, composing unity
From spin, so that its hollow spaces seem
Solids of light, until it wobbles and
Begins to whine, and then with an odd lunge
Eccentric and reckless, it skids away
And drops dead into its own skeleton.

Playing Skittles

No matter how dull your soul, you cannot help
But fill these skittering wooden dervishes
With spirit and will as you lean over their box
To watch them skip and weave and stagger among
The dumbbell pins. You even urge them on
Their drunken courses, cursing them when they miss
With what looks like purposeful malevolence,
Although you know they are like two blind men
Shut in invisible revolving doors—

With spirit and will and, yes, with mind as well:
They seem to go where they've a mind to go,
Sometimes intent, sometimes indifferent,
Until they stutter out of energy
And tumble over and lie down and die.

Of course they know no mind, and cannot mind
Either your prayers and curses or the pins.
And yet this matter of mind's no simple matter:
If not out there, then how in the world in here?
Agelong these tops concealed the gyroscope
Whose insane energies stabilize the earth.

TV

It would have delighted Bishop Berkeley by
Seeming to understand and demonstrate
What no one could refute by kicking stones,
The one dependency that links the mind
The senses and the world: whatever is made
The object of your vision is so made
Because another is looking at it too,
A fraction of a second earlier.

The straying lens across the battlefield,
The cameraman's quivering hand considering death,
The instant replay—all of them shopworn,
All soiled and secondhand goods of this world
Shaken in God's wavering attention just
An instant before we see it as out there.

The Spy

Out there, out there beyond the air,
Among the maelstroms of the burning dust,
The giant blue fires of the far away,
Beyond the eye of Palomar, out there
The witnessing astronomers go,
Lords of the Book of Zero.

Under the feet, under the solid ground,
The inaccessible burning of the earth
Makes whirlpools of the boiling rock,
Shifting the surface of the stable scene
And varying the mountains and the seas
Under the histories.

Behind the brow, a scant deep inch away,
The little nutshell mystery meditates
The spiral fire of the soul;
Through eyes as innocent and wide as day
It spies upon the true appearances of
Our sensible old world.

The Old Days*

Remember how Daylight Saving used to end
Near Halloween, just at the fall of leaf
When all the gardens died, All Saints, All Souls,
Those solemn first few days of getting used
To the sudden darkness bringing winter down
On all the grown-ups driving home from work,
The children kicking home through drifts of leaf?

This year the hour lost will stay away,
Kept out of time in some space of its own.
Will those who die fall sixty minutes short
Of what was owed? Where is that hour now,
What is its weather, is it dark or day?

*Reader, the Congress crossed us up about this one,
Which puts it with the missing hour in some gone
Dimension of the metaphysical playpen
Where whatever wasn't going to happen didn't happen.

102

Aftermath

When he had carried to term the sacred poem
That for so many years had starved him lean,
What in the world was left for him to do
In the world but wait there, in the world?

Now see him coming down Can Grande's stair
To eat Can Grande's bread, the wasted man
Who has been through Hell and seen what was to see,
And been through Heaven and seen what was to see,

And now is waiting for what is to be
Again, the second death although of bliss
Assured with his immortal girl restored—
Like Lazarus, save in his being saved.

The world is what it was: though Boniface
Is dead, so is the Savior-Emperor
(of typhoid, at Trier, all those years ago);
The world is what it always is; the Po

Is still a filthy ditch along whose banks
A populace of hogs, curs, wolves, pursues
Destruction as it did; nothing has changed,
The sacred poem is done, that heaven and earth

Had put their hands to, and like one lost he waits
Among the lost, musing sometimes on Virgil
In Limbo, and, though of bliss at last assured,
On how the Terrace of the Proud awaits

The painful penitent stooped under his stone.
Of all this, one imagines, he says nothing,
The man that mothers frighten children with:
"Be good, or he'll haul you back with him to Hell."

The Banquet

A translation of Dante Alighieri's *Convito,*
Dissertation 2, Canzone 1

Ye intelligences, turning the third sphere,
Hear out the reasoning within my heart
Stranger than I can openly relate.
The heaven that obeys your moving art
—Such noble natures as you surely are—
I see has brought me to my present state;
So of my suffering any debate
Seems that it rightly should be told to ye:
Wherefore I pray that ye will hear my part.
I would tell the strange history of the heart,
How the sad soul there weeps bitterly
Because a spirit speaks, opposing her,
That comes upon the shining of your star.

My sorrowful heart's life often would be
A thought so sweet that it would rise in flight
Many a time to the feet of our great Sire
To see a Lady glorious in light,
Of whom it spoke so blessedly to me
That my soul spoke, and said: "I would go there."
But, putting her to flight, one does appear
Who lords it with such power over me,
My trembling heart shows outwardly its fear.
And this one made me see a Lady here,
And said: "Who would behold felicity,
Let him look in this Lady's eyes
If he fears not the agony of sighs."

Now comes the adversary, who can slay,
Against my humble thought that would give me
Word of an angel crownéd in the skies,
So that my soul cried out, and still must cry,
Saying: "Alas, how is she fled away,
The piteous one who showed my pity's guise."
Then this afflicted heart said of its eyes:
"What hour such a lady looked therein,
Why would they not believe my word of her?"
Always I said: "In such eyes as hers are
One surely stands whose glance can murder men.
It not availed me, that I saw it plain,
Against their gazing whereby I am slain."

"You are not slain, but only as though blind,
Soul in our keeping, with so great lament,"
A spirit of gentle love replied to me.
"Because, upon that Lady all intent,
The life has so been driven from your mind
That you are full of fear, and cowardly.
But she is pity and humility,
Courteous and wise in her magnificence:
Know that she is your Lady from this day!
And having undeceived your eyes you may
See such high miracles her ornaments
That you will say to Love: O my true Lord,
Behold thy handmaid, who will do thy word."

Song, I think they will be few indeed
Who well and rightly understand your sense,
So difficult your speech and intricate.
Wherefore if you should come by any chance
Among such folk so little fit to read
As that you seem not to *communicate,*
I'd have you take heart even at that rate,
My latest and dear one, saying to them:
"Look you at least how beautiful I am."

An Ending

After the weeks of unrelenting heat
A rainy day brings August to an end
As if in ceremony. The spirit, dry
From too much light too steadily endured,
Delights in the heavy silver water globes
That make change from the sun's imperial gold;
The mind, relieved from being always brilliant,
Goes forth a penitent in a shroud of grey
To walk the sidewalks that reflect the sky,
The line of lights diminishing down the street,
The splashed lights of the traffic going home.

Origin

I went way back and asked the old
Ones deep in the graves, the youngest dead,
How language began, and who had the cred-
it of it, gods, men, devils, elves?
And this is the answer I was told:
"We got together one day," they said,
"And talked it over among ourselves."

Plane

The wingéd shadow with the self within,
Image projected at infinity,
Caught in the sky-completed rainbow's eye
And haloed in the gunsight of the sun,
Cruises beneath its substance, one on one.